"IF I DON'T TELL YOU, YOU WON'T KNOW!"

Drama, chuckle & heartache in the life of a joiner on the District Nurses Evening Service

Ben Parbold

To Maatha

Best Wishes

Ben Parbold

Copyright © 2020 Ben Parbold

All rights reserved.

ISBN: 9798577894962

DEDICATION

These stories are dedicated to carers for the ailing and the dying. May we all be fortunate in those who will care for us when our time comes.

CONTENTS

Acknowledgements i
1 From hanging doors to dressing sores 1
2 Sandy and the Jehovah's Witness 10
3 All the lonely people … 15
4 The night Sarah died 20
5 You really couldn't make it up 27
6 The Prestonshire Hillbillies 33
8 The blanket and the eiderdown 45
9 A Winter's Tale 51
10 The Times They Are a-Changing 54
11 "If I don't tell you, you won't know" 62
12 Just when you thought the night was over! 66
13 Parting thoughts 71
14 Retirement 75
Post Script 77

ACKNOWLEDGMENTS

None of this would have been possible but for my wife, Louise, her surprising suggestion that I should become an auxiliary nurse and her constant love and support.

Thanks a million, Louise.

Then there are the many wonderful, dedicated nurses I had the honour to work alongside. They taught me so much and not just about nursing.

I can't forget the patients and their families and carers. They showed me how important it is to appreciate every day.

Thanks to Daisy, Edward and Diane for the illustrations, to Frank for suggesting that my stories were worth writing down and for helping me to refine them and to Tina Konstant for patient and practical help with getting into print.

.

1 FROM HANGING DOORS TO DRESSING SORES

My nursing career would never have started but for Louise, my wife, who was a district nurse herself when we first met. I am a time-served joiner and I was running my own building company when she enrolled on my martial arts class at the YMCA in Westport. But that's a different story. The stories collected here are mostly about a joiner who became a nurse and his experiences on the West Prestonshire District Nurses Evening Service. And none of it would have happened without Louise … or the VAT man, come to that. He played his part too and I am thankful to them both.

I was doing well with the building. I had a small squad of tradesmen I'd grown up with and we worked well together, doing good work and growing a sound reputation. I loved it. I was busy enough and I knew what I was doing so there was no stress, apart from the VAT. That all came to a head when the inspector paid his annual visit to check my returns.

We fell out over missing invoices from the company I used for putting in damp courses. Trouble was, their invoice came as the guarantee, so I had to pass that on to the customer. I know I should have probably had a separate invoice from them as well but I only had that guarantee.

So he asked me, the VAT man,

> "Why isn't there an invoice from the damp coursing firm on your skewer with the rest of your invoices?"

> "Because," I explained, "I had to pass the guarantee, which was all together with the invoice, on to the customer but I have proof of payment. I have my cheque stubs and bank statements."

> "No! I want an invoice on the skewer."

> "But you know I've paid him."

I had my ledger with my 'in' and my 'out' and in my 'out' I had, 'Silver Thistle Damp Coursing Company', so much VAT, 'Paid'.

It was outrageous, really. Forty years later I'm still angry about it. I think if I'd had loads of money and a barrister to fight it and give him some stick, I probably would've won. But I didn't have the money to do that. So …

"If I don't tell you, you won't know!"

"No, no! If you've ..."

"Look! You know I've paid him. There's my check stub. There's my bank statement, in front of you."

"No! I want it on your skewer, an invoice with the rest of your invoices, so what I'm going to do, I'm going to re-bill you for every damp course job."

I think it was 15% VAT then, on top of my quarterly return. It was ruthless. Right out of order.

I said, "You can't do that!"

He said, "Yes I can!"

So he did and to my usual quarterly return there was another five hundred pounds added on. And he listed it, 'Silver Thistle, no invoice. Silver Thistle, no invoice, VAT on that job, to Ben Parbold, Joiner.'

It was outrageous. So, closing the door behind him that

day, I thought, 'Enough! Every week I spend Thursday evenings, keeping everything up to date, in my own time, at my own expense. I've been an unpaid tax collector for Her Majesty's Revenue and Customs for so many years and they don't even appreciate it.'

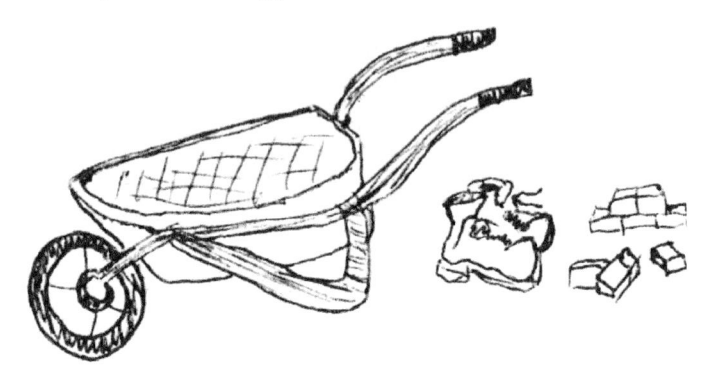

In those days I was collecting about three thousand pounds a quarter for them, for nothing and their relentless pressure and penalties made me realise that it was just not worth it. The stress was starting to affect my health. So I folded up the business.

You can see, it gets me going still, even now but it gives me great satisfaction to say that he hasn't had a penny from me since and I am so grateful for the amazing new life he helped to pitch me into.

But for then, back in 1991, I was left, casting about at a loose end, wondering what to do next and that's where Louise came in.

"I think you'd make a good auxiliary nurse," she said.

The thought: 'Me? Ben, the joiner? A nurse?' It filled me with dread but Louise set about writing to all the local hospitals. It was actual writing in those days too, no

Internet and soon after, I was invited for an interview at the Westport and Frimley District General Hospital and to keep her happy, I went along. 'There's no way they'll entertain a joiner working as an auxiliary nurse,' I thought.

My interview was with three kind nursing sisters, dressed in smart, blue uniforms.

"Would you like to start in two weeks?" they asked and showed me where to collect my uniform.

"Thank you very much," I said, in a state of total shock.

I had a two-week induction, attending courses and meeting all sorts of people before being thrown into the deep end on the male surgical ward of the Westport and Frimley District General Hospital.

In fact, I soon had two jobs. I was also working in community homes for people with special needs, more as a support worker than a nurse but it was useful because it gave me a grounding in the basics of care. I was registered on 'the bank', meaning I didn't have regular shifts. They just called me when they needed someone to fill in. So I was registered on the bank at the hospital and also with the community homes.

Now for the hospital, my employer was Westport and Frimley Health Authority but for the community homes, it was West Prestonshire Health Authority. That's who I ended up working for, years later, on the District. It was quite good really, being on the bank for two separate employers. It meant that if I was in the middle of something on a job of my own when the hospital rang up, I could say,

"Sorry, I'm at the community homes."

If the community homes rang up, I could say,

"Sorry, I'm at the hospital."

So I had three jobs going really … but getting back to my first day at Westport and Frimley General, there I was on the male surgical ward, in my new, white uniform, with the charge nurse asking me to go round the beds and change the patients' drips.

I had to take him to one side and explain,

"Terry, I'm a joiner. I've never done this before."

"Well don't let this lot know!"

It does sound bad to me now, looking back. "Don't let this lot know you're a joiner!" I mean, it was 'op' day and they were coming back from theatre. Elderly men with catheters, the irrigation flushing blood from their bladders into catheter bags. It put the fear of God up me. I'd expected to start on an ordinary ward, with bedmaking and bedpans but I was in at the deep end: the male surgical ward on op day … especially when it was only me and him! And with me thinking, 'Oh my lord ….'

Anyway, that's how it was, nearly forty years ago.

"Don't worry, Ben. You'll be fine. Just get on with it. But don't tell 'em you're a joiner."

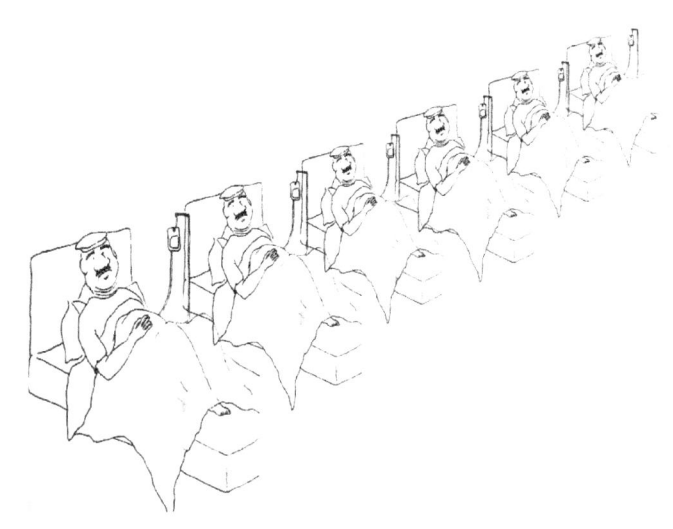

And once I started, I realised. It was very basic. Terry wasn't being reckless with patients' lives. I didn't even have to touch anyone, just shut off the flow, hang up a new bag and switch over.

An hour later, I couldn't remember what I was worrying for and that's roughly how it went for the next eight years. It was like serving my apprenticeship all over again ... but I had no idea it was preparing me for the job of my life on the West Prestonshire District Nurses Evening Service.

That began when I spotted a vacancy for an auxiliary on the Evening Service. It was the shift pattern that caught my eye: seven pm until midnight. Our daughter was just one year old at the time, so we thought that would be ideal. I could take care of Penny during the day, while Louise was at her nursing job and then she could take over at night.

So I applied, went for another rigorous interview, took the

phone call the same evening to hear I had been successful and four weeks later, I was on the District.

Who'd have thought, on that dark night in November 1991, as I set out on my first shift, that I had such a life changing experience ahead of me? How could I have known it would be such a privilege? At the time, of course, I was nervous, going out to meet a new team of colleagues and to start learning a new job but when I look back on that day, it gets me tingling with gratitude and excitement.

In those days we worked from seven until midnight and we were known as 'The Twilight Nurses'. Two teams of four nurses organised into two shifts covered the seven nights of the week for all of West Prestonshire, with two auxiliaries and two staff nurses in each team.

For the first few years, there was no nursing cover once we were finished. So if any calls or referrals came in during the evening, from A&E or from the GPs, we'd add them to our list and carry on until all the patients had been seen to, even though our shift - and our pay - ended at midnight. Getting home after one or two in the morning was quite a normal occurrence and we didn't think twice about it.

Then in the mid-nineteen nineties an all night service was set up to ensure twenty four hour availability of district nurses, covering from the end of our shift until the day-staff came on the following morning. So any extra patients referred during the evening could be passed on to the all night nurses and we were able to finish on time every night.

We couldn't believe it and thought all our birthdays had come at once. But looking back, there was something special about those early years. I always had a sense of real satisfaction, driving home in the early hours, half asleep, going over how we'd got through it all again. It was like the patients were really ours. They depended on us. We had to see they were set for the night, reassured, comfortable and free from pain, until the nurses on the daytime service came around in the morning.

I worked with many wonderful nurses over the years and even one or two who were not so wonderful. You get all sorts in all professions and nursing turns out to be no different. Mostly, I worked with Ann and Val and we developed the closest of bonds. Val even joked about me being her second husband … and she was still happily married to her first. Together, we took care of many, many people during the last few months and weeks of their lives, for some even, the last few minutes. There were so many extraordinary moments and I couldn't have hoped for better people to go through them with.

Of course, my other companions along this amazing, twenty-year journey were the patients and their relatives and friends, some of the bravest and most interesting people I ever knew. I would like to introduce some of them through these stories as a tribute to them all and to the dedicated nurses I had the honour to work alongside.

So let the stories begin. Twenty years! Two decades. So many stories, funny and sad, chuckle and heartache, human stories, people being people, vulnerable and resilient, many at the end of their lives. It really was such a privilege.

2 SANDY AND THE JEHOVAH'S WITNESS

Sandy was originally from Glasgow. We visited her over a long period and came to love the grand stories she told in her broad Scottish accent. She could swear like a trooper but she had a heart of gold. She always had sweets and chocolates for us from her big tin of Quality Street and at Christmas time, she'd give us a tin of our own for a present to take back and enjoy at the office.

She suffered from COPD (chronic obstructive pulmonary disease) and she had oxygen cylinders by her bed for when she needed help with her breathing but it never stopped her puffing on her cigarettes. I just laugh when I think of her. When we visited we could hear the sound of the TV long before we went into the house.

Her husband had a problem with his hearing and had to have the sound full on. It was deafening. We would have asked him to turn it down but he couldn't hear a word we said. So there was a lot of shouting as we all tried to understand each other.

Even with her serious condition, she went back to Glasgow to visit her sister every year. Can you imagine? The oxygen by her bed was only for emergencies, in case she had a bad attack but even so! Every year she'd leave it behind, set out for the station on her own and wheeze her way up to Scotland on the bus. She was that feisty, was Sandy. She cracked us up. What a will! What a personality!

She always went on her own, leaving her husband behind and it was while she was away on one of these visits that he had a fatal heart attack and died. So Sandy was left to cope on her own but at least the house was much quieter now, without the TV full on and she seemed to manage perfectly well, for a while.

Eventually, after some quiet months alone, she started to

think it would be nice to have a little pet for company. Asking about, she soon found some kittens and puppies needing a home and in no time, she had a tiny kitten and a Jack Russell pup. She also came to hear of a lady offering a baby's swinging crib and thought it would be ideal for her new pets to sleep in.

Sandy was never shy about calling for help when she needed it, so she asked the lady with the crib if she might deliver it to the house which she kindly did. Waiting patiently after ringing the bell, the lady was startled when an elderly invalid, wreathed in a haze of cigarette smoke, opened the door. She thought she'd come to the wrong house.

'Nae', said Sandy. 'It's no' for a baby. It's for ma wee kitten an' ma pup.'

The lady could see her cradle was going to a good home. She was glad and it always cheered us too, in the middle of a long shift, to drop in on Sandy and see the two pets curled up happily together in their swinging crib.

As I said, she was never shy about asking for help and would often phone us to say the light bulb had gone in the lounge or the toilet and could we stop by to put in a new one? Even though we were always rushed off our feet, we usually managed to be passing by at some point and find time to bob in for two minutes to change the bulb for her, although once, it was about her washing machine.

"It's broken doon. Would you be any guid wi' that?"

We had to draw a line there and let her down as tactfully as we could.

"Sorry, Sandy. We can't stretch to washing machine repairs."

My favourite story, of the many Sandy told us over the

years, was about a Jehovah's Witness who came for tea. She had a friend who knew someone at the local Kingdom Hall and would Sandy like her to ask him to call for a chat? She thought it might be nice to have some company to talk to and a few days later, a Jehovah's Witness rang the bell.

> "Come in. You're very welcome," said Sandy, opening the door. "Sit yersel' doon. Would you like a nice cup o' tea or coffee and a piece o' cake?"

> "That would be lovely," said the gentleman. "I'll have tea, please, no sugar, just milk. And cake would be lovely. Thank you very much."

They were happily chatting away to each other until Sandy lit a cigarette and the man's face fell.

> "Oh dear, Sandy!" said the Jehovah's Witness. "You shouldn't be doing that in your condition!"

This didn't go down at all well with Sandy.

> "You know how a few moments ago I said you were very welcome? Well your nae fukn' welcome any mair!"

And the Jehovah's Witness was hurried to the door. He probably never understood he was dealing with such a woman: such a golden heart and such a powerful personality. She was admitted to hospital shortly afterwards and we soon heard she had passed away.

Rest in peace, Sandy.

Ben Parbold

3 ALL THE LONELY PEOPLE …

Mary was an elderly patient who had never married and lived on her own in Ormsley. We visited her every evening to put clean dressings on her ulcerated leg. After each visit, she never failed to ask if we were OK for teabags for back at the office when we finished our shift and however we answered, she always insisted we have a packet of Rington's teabags to take back with us.

Well, after several months of visiting Mary, we had an abundance of teabags back at the office and certainly never went short of a nice cup of tea at the end of the shift. So one evening, I followed her into her kitchen to say, how kind it was of her,

"... but Mary we don't want you going short of teabags for yourself."

"Don't worry," she said, opening every cupboard door in her kitchen. "I won't go short."

I looked all round in amazement. Every shelf, in every

cupboard, top to bottom was stacked with boxes of Rington's teabags.

"I like to buy a packet from the nice young man who delivers them every week because he stops and chats with me."

That was the moment I realised, I wasn't standing there with just another kindly old lady, dishing out tea. I was standing with a desperately lonely woman. It was quite a moment. It shook me.

Now, don't get me wrong. I loved that job because of all the people I met while I was doing it. I love people. Louise will tell you, I'll talk to anyone. (Actually, she'll say, I'd talk a glass eye to sleep.) But I have to be honest, on a normal shift, there wasn't much time to chat.

Flying round, all over West Prestonshire, every night, with a list of ten or twelve calls to make, it can be easy to fall into a habit of treating every kindly, grey-haired spinster like any other. In the middle of life and death, we'd have safe conversations about the weather, nice cups of tea, looking on the bright side and so on.

But that evening, following Mary into the kitchen, was altogether different. I thought she was just opening a cupboard to show me she had plenty of tea but instead, she hit me with that.

I stared in amazement at all her boxes and boxes of tea. She always bought a packet, every week, from the nice young man, no matter what. I could see what his visit meant to her, how she looked forward to it in a week that didn't have too many bright spots.

It was a small experience with Mary that evening, so simple, the simplest thing under the sun. But bringing real life to the front, realising what people are going through and what's happening out there, it was also huge. It's one of the most memorable moments of my twenty years with the Service.

§§§

Although most of our patients were receiving terminal care, we also had minor visits, to administer drops, for example, for post-op patients after eye surgery. They were mainly elderly folk, living alone without anybody to help them with their treatment. Alex was one of these patients and another lonely old soul. All his life he'd lived with his mum and worked in the parks and gardens department for West Prestonshire Council. After she passed away, he was left in the family home to cope by himself which he managed to do quite adequately.

Each evening, on our visit, we'd be greeted as we went through the door.

"Huh! I might have known it would be you!"

It seemed to us, if there had been an award for the grumpiest person in Britain, Alex would have been winning it year after year. This just summed him up.

He had an elderly lady friend he used to visit for Sunday lunch. So when we saw him we'd ask,

"Did you have a nice lunch with your lady friend on Sunday?"

"Huh!" he'd reply, "Lettuce on bread!"

"Nothing else?"

"Taters!"

"Nothing else?" ... and he'd go,

"Meeatt!" in an angry and grumpy manner.

He even said the word 'meat' so grumpily.

When we visited once around Christmas time, Alex was wearing a new jumper.

"Is that lovely new jumper a Christmas present from your lady friend, Alex," we'd ask?

"Huh! Yes. But in two weeks time it won't be new, will it? Huh!"

We called on Alex for quite a few weeks, almost every day. We'd spend just those brief moments with him, giving him his drops, making friendly conversation and smiling at his unexpected remarks. What did he sound like?

We laughed but not unkindly. Over the weeks and months, through these small daily dealings, we got to know him and grew fond of him. For all his grumpy, rude, unappreciative remarks, we knew there was no harm in him. It was just Alex.

"If I don't tell you, you won't know!"

"… and the West Prestonshire Grumpy Award 2008 goes to … Alex Harwood!"

4 THE NIGHT SARAH DIED

On the night Sarah died, the two nurses on the other team of our shift were already at the office when I arrived.

"There's a message from James on the ansaphone," said Bridget.

James and Sarah were a young couple who lived together in a tidy, terraced cottage beside the Woolcity - Seaport Canal, where it goes through Winsbridge. We didn't know them very well as they were quite independent and seldom needed any help from the Evening Service. Mostly, our daytime colleagues took care of them but we knew who they were and we knew Sarah was dying.

Although she was only in her late twenties, she had cancer and AIDS and was very poorly. The message was from James, saying he was going with her and he'd taken all her tablets. Val had been first into the office, picked up the message and gone straight to their home.

"I'd better get after her," we agreed which left Bridget and Pam adding some of our patients to their list.

Later, we had to ring them and they ended up taking our whole night's work but at that point, we had no idea what we were in for.

So how did it start? I arrived and James was saying,

> "There's no point ringing an ambulance. There's no way I'm leaving her. I'm going with her, wherever she goes."

We knew he was full of tablets. Val was feeding him hot milk and keeping him talking and awake. He knew Sarah was close to dying. The day staff would probably have warned him what to expect. He sat with her, holding her and we listened to her irregular breathing. Near the end, there's a pattern you can recognise, called Cheyne-Stoking. It's a sort of gasp, followed by some shorter breaths and then a pause before the next gasp, with the pauses gradually getting longer.

And then, soon, her breathing stopped. She died and the room went quiet. Val took her pulse.

> "She's gone, James."

We didn't know anything of their story, how such a young woman came to be taken by those dreadful diseases but we could see that James was devoted to her. He made a good job of looking after her and he kept the home in good order. Some of the places we have to go can be pretty grim but it was obvious that there was love and care in this home.

After a moment, he moved away, leaving us to get on with the familiar nursing procedures; removing her catheter, taking down the syringe-driver that had been administering her drugs, leaving her comfortable and peaceful for James.

He was very upset, distraught. So Val said,

"Look, James, I know you don't want to leave her, if you want to lie with her for a while, there's no harm in that. Just stay with her."

That appeared to pacify him, he didn't seem particularly unwell and even slept a little, so everything was fine, for the time being.

Our next job was to phone the GP to come and certify the death and then contact the undertaker as James wasn't in a fit state to do any of this for himself.

"Is there anybody we can contact for you, James? Relatives or friends? To come and be with you? Or just to let them know?"

"Don't ring me mum and dad!" he said. "I hate them!"

They were living in Seaport, both alcoholics, apparently. James explained that while he was still living at home, each evening after school, he and his brother had to go to the off-licence and carry a crate of cider back to the house and then go upstairs to their bedroom and keep out the way.

"So whatever you do, don't ring me mum and dad! But there's my brother. He's a taxi driver now, in Hendridge. You could call him."

So we called James's brother and explained the situation. He said he'd come right away and indeed, arrived shortly after but *with* the mum and dad in the cab. (Oh dear!) Hardly were they in the door but James and his father were shouting at each other and fighting. So there we were, trying to break up a fight, more bouncers at a night club than district nurses on their round, bearing in mind, all the while, poor Sarah was lying dead in her bed.

The situation quickly got that bad, we told the parents

that we really thought it would be better if they went and we managed to talk them into leaving. James's mother asked if she could just say her goodbyes to her daughter-in-law, which she did and then, they went away in the taxi. (Phew! What a relief!) But the respite didn't last very long.

After the fight with his dad and the whole situation with his parents, we could soon see that James was all wound up and agitated. So he decided, to prevent matters getting any worse, that what he really needed was to get along to the off-licence for a few cans of lager.

"I've got to have a drink," he said.

"Look, James," I said, "you can't drive in your condition."

"Yes, I can!" he said, insistently. "I'm going to anyway."

In desperation I decided to offer him a lift myself and luckily, just as we were going out the back door, the GP arrived.

"Oh James! Here's the GP. He'll want to talk to you. We'll have to go back in," which we did and that was another close shave.

The GP examined Sarah, spoke to James and wrote the death certificate. He was one of the local Asian GPs we used to see regularly on our visits. He came over to Val and I on his way out.

"You know, you've got a very tricky situation here."

"You don't say!" I said, "You haven't seen the half of it … before you came!" and he left.

So that was the GP and now we were waiting for the undertaker, alone again with James. He was still agitated and ready for throwing himself in the canal so we kept talking, kept on with the hot milk and explained that the undertaker would soon be here and wanting to talk to him.

"They're not taking her," he said. "They're not taking her anywhere!" (Oh dear.)

The young undertaker came soon after and sat down with James, speaking so calmly and kindly.

"Tomorrow you'll be able to come to the chapel and you'll be able to see her, James. She'll be beautiful. We'll make her lovely for you."

We could see the effect his kind, gentle way of speaking was having on James as he calmed down and became more relaxed. So they brought the trolley in, lifted Sarah onto it and we all followed, along the narrow path to the van, keeping James on the inside, away from the canal.

We watched as they lifted her into the van. The undertaker shook James by the hand, explaining that he would phone the next day to arrange a time for him to visit the chapel and we watched the van drive away. James and I walked back to the cottage along the canal path. I was still mindful of his unstable mood and how easily we might still all end up in the water but it didn't happen.

"If I don't tell you, you won't know!"

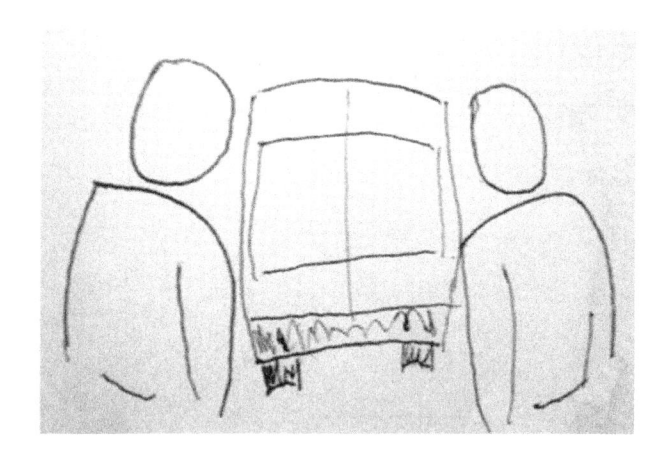

We were soon safely back in the cottage for more hot milk where we managed to talk James into letting us take him to A&E and after all the trauma of the evening, he was happy to go. We all went in Val's car so I could sit in the back with James to keep him awake and talking.

"What do you think you might do in the future, James?" I asked him.

"There's a Buddhist monastery I know in the Lake District," he replied. "I'm going there."

It seems he had prepared himself.

"What a wonderful thing to do, James" I agreed. "I wish you all the luck with that."

I often wonder if he went. I hope so.

We left him in the good hands of the doctors and nurses at A&E and went back for my car in a daze. I got home at 3am. We had been with them our whole shift. We found out later they had pumped James's stomach and he was fine. But the scenarios that unfolded that night, one after the other, were unbelievable. I don't think I've remembered it all here but I will never forget James and Sarah. There are some things that never leave you.

5 YOU *REALLY* COULDN'T MAKE IT UP

Looking back, I can hardly believe these stories myself. The variety of people and their situations, our little snapshots into their lives as we called in on them, one by one, side by side, all in the same county.

One evening, Val and I had been making single patient visits, so we were working independently, each in our own car. Sometimes only one nurse is needed but for Peter, an old patient in West Rigby, we had to double-up.

He was a big man with a degenerative condition that was steadily reducing his mobility and he wasn't accepting it graciously. He kept himself going for years, thanks to an iron will, significant personal wealth and a family that had been drilled into putting his needs ahead of their own. He could be aggressive and demanding, a bully, to be honest but he was our patient and it was our responsibility to provide him with the care he needed.

I'd got the measure of him, over the years and I could manage him well enough but none of us enjoyed going in and some of the nurses were quite afraid of him. So that's why Val and I were arriving outside his home in our separate cars. After a brief chat, we went in together, saw to his care, without incident and were back outside again in no time.

We were just getting into our cars when a GP called, on Val's phone, to request a home visit for one of her patients. She waved me over so we could speak about how we were going to fit the extra patient in and I left my car, with the door open, to go over. That's obviously how the cat got in but I didn't realise until I was a hundred yards up the road when I looked in the rear view mirror and saw it on the parcel shelf.

All wide-eyed and bristling after realising it was on the move and heading away from home, it started to panic and run round the car, over my shoulders, across the dashboard and back again. My first chance to turn around was the pub car park at the top of the road. Back at the patient's house, I let the distraught cat out of the car and knocked at the door to explain that he must have jumped in while we were speaking to the GP.

> "I've taken your cat to the pub, Peter and if he's a good boy, next week, I'll take him to the cinema."

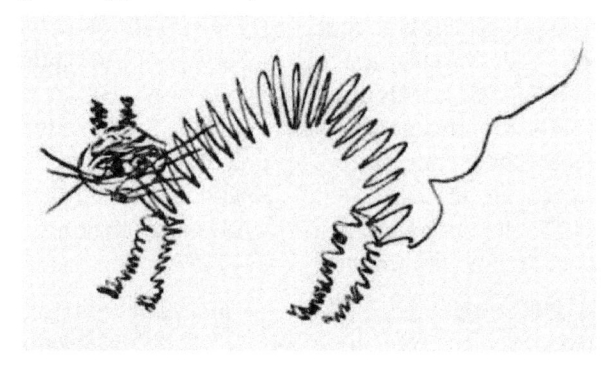

Little incidents like that often helped me through a difficult visit during a long shift, especially when I had a sympathetic companion to laugh with afterwards. I count myself lucky to have started working with Val early on in my time on the District. She ended up being my staff nurse partner for most of the next fifteen years, the kindest, warmest and most professional nurse you could ever hope to meet. On top of all that, she was a wonderful singer as well. What more would you want from a colleague?

Every evening for some months, Val and I visited Tom and Sally. Tom was our patient and Sally was his wife. Tom had worked as a landscape gardener all his life and was as strong as an ox. His condition was a form of dementia which sometimes led to him becoming aggressive and it was my role to hold down his hands while Val, with the help of Sally, attended to his personal hygiene.

We found it made all our lives easier if we could find a way to distract him and the best way we found was singing. Even though his dementia had taken away his speech, he could still join in with, "Ho-di-ho, ho-di-ho," at the top of his voice and for most of our visit we'd be singing along with Tom and Sally. (It brings back lovely memories, thinking about them.)

One evening while we were attending to him, he startled us. We'd only ever heard him sing, "Ho-di-ho, ho-di-ho." But suddenly, he shouted out,

"Four! Six! Seven!"

Sally, Val and I looked at each other.

"I'll put those numbers along with Tom's date of birth on the lottery," I said.

I used to organise a little syndicate with all the nurses each week. If you're waiting to hear how we scooped the top prize with Tom's numbers, like us, you'll be disappointed. Not a sausage in twenty years. But it's been a fun way to remember Singing Tom and Sally.

§§§

We mostly worked together with the same nurses in the same teams but if a colleague was on annual leave or off sick we would often help each other out, covering for each other for short spells. That's how we came to meet Eileen, an auxiliary nurse from our opposite shift. She was covering for our Bridget who was unwell.

It was the first night after changeover. We'd been off the night before while Eileen had been working with her usual team. As we were getting together our list of patients, Eileen asked me if we were going to see Billy and his wife.

"Yes," I said, "He's on our list for a visit. We haven't been before so it'll be our first time."

"I was at Billy's last night with my team," she said, "and you will not believe his tattoos!"

"What d'you mean, Eileen?"

"You will not believe where he has his tattoos!"

"Where, Eileen? For goodness sake!"

"Well ... make sure you pay attention to his privates!"

Eileen would often tell a good story so we thought she was winding us up but I have to admit, she had me intrigued. Anyway, Val and I set out on our visits and were soon busy enough to think no more of it until we got to Billy's house. Even there, it was hardly the first thing on our minds.

"If I don't tell you, you won't know!"

Billy was very poorly. His condition was a cancer of the brain which had progressed to a stage where he was no longer conscious. He had to have a permanent catheter and we set about attending to his personal hygiene and checking his pressure areas when ... there they were. We couldn't believe our eyes. Eileen had not been winding us up.

Two beautiful love birds, in intricate detail, tattooed in colour, one on each testicle, a complete work of art and down the length of his penis, a woman's first name. We couldn't imagine how on earth he could have withstood it. The pain! How did he go through with it? Was he drunk at the time? He was of an age with my Dad, so probably in one of the armed forces during the Second World War. My Dad also came home with tattoos, although not on his penis, so far as I know.

Sadly, Billy didn't last much longer. He died a couple of days later, before we were able to find out the name of his wife and whether it was their loving relationship commemorated by his tattoos. They've all gone now so we'll never know but the question still pops into my mind from time to time.

6 THE PRESTONSHIRE HILLBILLIES

As I've said, my wife has also been a district nurse. It was what she was doing when we first met and she told me some wonderful stories as we sat in the evenings and chatted about our days and this is one of hers.

The area she covered was also very rural, like mine. So she was often visiting patients who were farmers. On this occasion it was Old Tommy and her visit to his farmhouse was to see to the dressings on his ulcerated legs. Tommy would sit in a chair, in his underpants, while Louise removed the old dressings and replaced them with fresh ones.

When she had finished he stood up and his underpants fell to the floor. They looked about four sizes too big for him as he had probably been wearing them since he'd been five stone heavier, several years before.

As she helped him to pull them up, Louise did her best to hide her dismay at the state of the dark grey underpants, soiled with brown streaks.

"Would you like me to put you on a nice clean pair, Tommy?" she asked him.

"Eee, nay, Lass. There's only me an't' wife."

Newly married herself, she was struck dumb! "Good grief! Is this what I've got to prepare myself for?!?!" Louise's mother used to howl at that story … the implications of that remark!

"There's only me an't' wife."

§§§

Oh my God, the lady with the torch! What a night that

was! And the trouble was, I was out with Kath, a nurse I didn't usually work with. I knew her well enough because she was the other staff nurse from our team but she usually worked with Vicky. Anyway, for some reason I can't remember now, Kath and I were working together and the trouble with Kath was, she wasn't always the most patient person in the world. In fact, she could be quite short and to make matters worse, she was the driver for the night. So to come across a visit like that with her was the perfect combination.

A large part of the area served by the West Prestonshire District Nurses is very rural with many patients who were market gardeners. On this particularly dark and bleak winter's night we were looking for an address somewhere along a four-mile stretch of straight, unlit lane, dotted with private bungalows and houses as well as farms and smallholdings. We had no house number, only the name of the grower displayed on a faded board.

We drove up and down the lane but we couldn't find the property or see any board with the name on so we rang the patient for directions and spoke to his wife.

"We can't see your signboard."

"No. It fell down a while ago."

"Ah. OK. Is there any other description you can give us to help us find you?"

"I could leave a light on for you in the front room?"

"OK. Thank you."

Well, it was soon obvious, as we drove up and down, that nearly every property had a light on in the front room. I can hear Kath now.

"Ring them again. Ring them. And keep her on the

phone this time!"

I could see it boiling up in her, the frustration.

"Perhaps you could go out and stand at the front of your property," I suggested, "so we can see you?"

"Right ho! I've got a torch. I'll do that."

On we drove, up and down the dark lane, straining our eyes for the light of a torch in the gloom. Eventually, I spotted a dark figure up a driveway and we stopped.

"Are you expecting a visit from the district nurses?"

"Yes we are," she replied.

"Are you the lady with the torch?"

"Aye," she said, holding it up, "but there weren't any batteries in it so I've just been standing in the driveway."

It's hard to believe, looking back, those isolated, rural lives, almost like our own hillbillies. I felt sorry for them really because Kath wasn't making any effort to conceal her frustration. She was a scouser and not afraid to speak her mind and she made it perfectly obvious she was none too happy about our wasted half hour.

Anyway, we'd found them at last and went in to attend to the patient. As we came out, his wife was stood with a big bag of potatoes and vegetables for each of us. We were glad enough to accept her peace offering and carry on with our visits. But I'm still chuckling now.

Ben Parbold

7 THE DRAMA, THE CHUCKLE AND THE HEARTACHE

Ah! Now this was another tough one, out of the blue, working with Doris that time. Doris was a bank nurse. The service keeps a list of nurses on 'the bank'. They may be called on when there aren't enough regular staff to fill the teams because of sickness or holidays, for example. I had worked with Doris as my staff nurse on many occasions over the years. Her day job was at a local hospice so she had a lot of experience with terminally ill patients and I always felt in good hands when I was working with her.

Our list that evening included a visit to a gentleman who lived in a lovely cottage in a small community out in the countryside. His condition required a syringe driver to administer his drugs continuously over a period of twenty-four hours. He slept in a downstairs bedroom and after attending to him, we went into the kitchen with his wife to write up the 'Nurses' Notes'.

Every visit we'd have to update the records that are kept in the house with the patient. It's for continuity with the ongoing care, mainly for the other team or any medical staff who might call, so they could see how things were going. Usually, the staff nurse wrote the notes while I chatted with the patient's wife or husband or whoever else might be there. It was always part of our job to keep an eye on how the family and any other carers were coping and if there was anything else we could do to support them. It was important because there were times when the carer could go down before the patient did.

So while Doris wrote up the notes, I was chatting with the patient's wife when the doorbell rang and she went to answer it, leaving us in the kitchen. All of a sudden, we heard a bit of a commotion and a scream. I ran out to find her on the floor, very distressed. She had a respiratory condition herself and was quite breathless as I helped her up. As I was getting her into a chair, Doris came to tell me there was a man stood at the foot of the patient's bed. So she took over with the wife while I went to see what was happening there.

The man turned out to be a son from a previous marriage. He was still there, stood at the end of the bed. It seems he had forced his way past the woman, who must have been his stepmother, somehow knocking her to the floor. He wanted to stay and talk but I said to him,

"Look. We'll have to report this to the police. She's been knocked to the floor. I think it would be better if you left."

"I only want to see my dad before he dies," he told us.

"Yeah, but you've knocked the lady to the floor. We've got to report this. We can't leave it."

He didn't stay long and it turned out, Doris had already phoned the police. While we waited for them, we were able to contact the lady's daughter. She lived nearby and soon arrived to comfort her mum.

When the police came they took statements from Doris and I and the patient's wife. By this time, her breathing had settled down and we were able to leave her with her daughter. We explained to the police that we would have to get on with our round as we still had many other patients to see and off we went.

About two weeks later I received a letter instructing me to attend Hendridge Magistrate's Court as a witness to the incident. It was pretty unnerving, being cross-examined by his solicitor who fired questions at me quite aggressively but I just said it as it was. I had to keep explaining. We'd been in the kitchen. I hadn't actually seen the incident. I didn't know how the woman ended up on the floor. I never saw the man knock her down. I only knew he had pushed his way in, obviously, because the woman didn't want him there but I didn't witness any assault. So the case was dismissed for lack of evidence and the man was acquitted.

Looking back, I never felt this was any great miscarriage of justice. Just another sad family situation got out of hand. Just another example of how we never knew, as we set out each evening, what the shift was going to throw at us. Who would have thought, out of a routine visit, I'd be drawn into the legal system and end up giving evidence in court?

§§§

Over the years, I became quite accustomed to the presence of death on this job but when it came for children, so much before their time, it was always hard.

So when we received a phone call from Cedar Grove Children's Hospital as Ann and I were in the office sorting our list of patients for the shift, we knew it would be a heavy one. Could we add another patient to our list: a twelve your old boy who was terminally ill? We were to call in, see how he was doing and make him comfortable for the night.

We were never normally asked to visit children because the hospital had their own pediatric palliative care team but on this occasion, they couldn't get to him and asked us to call. To make matters worse, Ann's son was being treated for leukemia in the same hospital at the same time. The other staff nurse on our team offered to take that visit but Ann said,

"No," as I knew she would, "I will be OK," and the young boy was added to our list.

On the way to the visit, I knew it would be difficult for Ann but I had no doubt she would handle it in her usual caring and professional way. I was more worried about how she would be afterwards.

The mother greeted us at the house and showed us to the young boy's room.

"The nurses are here for you, Sam," she said.

Sam lifted his head from the pillow and said, "Hello," in a frail voice.

Then mum left us to it and we set about checking Sam's drugs and pain control and making him as comfortable as we could for the night. He gave a little groan as we lifted him up the bed as gently as we could but never once complained. We said goodnight to Sam and went downstairs to write our notes while chatting with his mum. She appeared to be very strong and composed.

"I've had to stay strong for Sam because his dad isn't coping very well," she said.

We stood there for a while, in front of this courageous woman, in total admiration of her resilience, knowing the sadness and heartache that was in front of her. We managed to maintain our composure until we set off to see our next patient. Too full of emotion to speak, neither of us said a word all the way, tears rolling down our cheeks. I was wondering about Ann. What was going through her mind about her son, his cancer, his treatment, his prospects? What a privilege to know them, I was thinking, such people as young Sam and his mother and Ann, my colleague and friend.

§§§

On a happier note, Ann's lad made a full recovery and was last reported well into his university studies. We had many laughs together too. Visiting a terminally ill patient, a lady, at her home in Belmerstone, for example. We arrived at the house to find rows of black Range Rovers and top-of-the-range BMWs with personalised number plates parked up in front. It definitely wasn't the sort of line up you'd expect to see outside a modest house in Blem.

Knocking at the door, a young man in his early twenties answered and invited us in. He led us through a room with a number of men in dark suits, all in their twenties and thirties and looking like the guests at a Blues Brothers fancy dress party. It was never my place to judge but I couldn't imagine how they managed to afford the astonishing array of smart cars outside. Each of the men must've had his own. I wondered if we'd stumbled on the local mafia clan.

"These are my brothers," he explained, leading us on

up the stairs to meet our patient in her bedroom.

Sat with her, in a chair beside the bed, was an older gentleman with a large, grey, bushy beard and a mass of grey hair who I took to be her husband.

The two men left us alone with our patient to give her the nursing care she needed and as we finished and went to go back downstairs, we passed the older one again. He had been waiting patiently on the upstairs landing and went straight back in to carry on sitting with her. With the concern he was showing, his body language and attitude, everything about him, it was obvious to me, he was her husband.

Back in the lounge, all the young men were gathered along with two teenagers on the settee. While Ann wrote up the notes, I was chatting with one of the sons.

"How's your Dad coping?" I asked him.

"Dad? Oh! Upstairs. That's not my Dad. He died ten years ago. That's our eldest brother."

"Oh!" I said, "and these will be his sons," nodding at the two teenagers on the settee who would have heard all our conversation.

"That's right," he replied.

("Whoops! Ann? Start the car!")

I apologised for having put my foot in it and we left them chuckling away amongst themselves.

The funny bit, though, was on the following evening. The same patient was on our list and when we knocked on the door a new man answered, with immaculate, jet-black hair and the most neatly trimmed, jet black beard. I quickly realised, of course, it was the same man, with the bushy grey hair and beard but he'd tidied himself up quite a bit.

"I'm sorry about the mix up last night," I said.

He shook my hand.

"Don't worry about it, lad. We all make mistakes," and we all laughed about it again.

Looking at his smart, new grooming with his jet-black hair and beard, all neatly trimmed, I felt we might have treated two patients in that household. I also saw another family, just another family, mothers and sons, navigating the choppy waters of family life and death.

8 THE BLANKET AND THE EIDERDOWN

This is another of my wife's stories and it still gives me the shivers whenever I think about it. It's about a strange coincidence and the importance of kindness.

During her career as a nurse, Louise went to Wincaster University to take a degree in health studies. After graduating she took a post with the NHS as a health visitor for our local area around Westport. One day she was visiting an elderly lady called Joyce who lived in a grim flat where she was pestered by other tenants in the property. Louise set to work on getting Joyce re-housed and eventually, she was able to move into a lovely, ground floor flat in a warden-controlled block.

Louise continued to call on Joyce from time to time, to see how she was keeping and to give her a bit of company and over the years, we learned more and more about her. Life had not been easy. As a young woman, she'd been married but her husband was abusive towards her and mistreated her. She stayed with him for a number of years until she was finally able to get out of the relationship and start again on her own.

Sometimes she spoke to Louise about her childhood, growing up in Seaport and working in her mother's flower shop. Once, she remembered looking out from the shop on a wet, wintry day and seeing a young girl walking past with a baby in a pram. Joyce had felt sorry for the young mum, thinking she looked so cold and miserable in the rain and ran out to say she had a warm blanket inside. Would she like it for the baby?

"Oh, yes please," said the girl. "Thank you for being so kind."

I can't really remember when she stopped being 'Little Joyce', the patient and became Joyce, the friend of the family. One Christmas day, for example, we took some turkey round and some Christmas pudding. We just kept popping in now and again, keeping an eye on her and getting to know her.

On one of our visits, Joyce surprised Louise by asking,

"When anything happens to me, I've no family to sort things out. Will you be my executor and deal with my flat?"

Louise reassured her that she would be only too glad and Joyce must not worry.

I'm a bit uneasy, looking back on it now. From the modern perspective of our more cynical world, there might be questions asked, about ethics and professional boundaries.

("Health workers take advantage of vulnerable old lady," goes the headline in the Daily Mail. "Over more than five years, scheming Louise Parbold, aided

by her partner Ben, (because it's always the woman's fault) wormed her way into the life of vulnerable Little Joyce Claridge.")

But at the time, it honestly never even occurred to us for a moment that there might have been anything improper about the situation. In fact, we were touched by her trusting us with such a responsibility and never gave it a second thought. We were all part of the same community, just looking out for each other.

Now I must introduce the other strand of this story, Louise herself had also been in receipt of great kindness. Her mother, May, had died recently, some fourteen months after being incapacitated by a stroke. During this time we acquired a new friend called Maureen. We had advertised for someone to keep May company while she was unwell, taking her out in a wheel chair now and again or just sitting in to chat. Maureen particularly liked spending time with elderly people and she turned out to be an ideal companion for May. In a similar way as with Louise and Joyce, as the months passed, we all became friends and our friendship with Maureen continued after May died.

Stopping by for a coffee and a chat one day, Maureen told Louise about another of her elderly friends, Mary, an independent and house-proud lady who lived alone, just over the road from Maureen. In her neighbourly way, she had started bobbing in to see if Mary was OK and to get bits of shopping for her. Like Louise and Joyce, Maureen was slowly hearing more and more stories from Mary's long life.

One of these stories, which Maureen had enjoyed enough to pass on to Louise, was of how, as a young mum, Mary had been pushing a pram past a local flower shop in Seaport one rainy day, when a kind girl had run out with a blanket for her baby.

Can you imagine? I get goose-pimples thinking about it even now. Louise was stunned, remembering the story she'd heard from Joyce a few years before. Could it be true that Maureen's friend Mary was the same young girl that had pushed her pram past Joyce's mum's flower shop in Seaport all those years ago? Seventy? Eighty years? When Louise told Joyce's side of the story to Maureen, they worked out that both old ladies were indeed of an age and from the same part of Seaport.

Sadly, Mary was in hospital at the time and Joyce died a few months later, just weeks short of her hundredth birthday. So there wasn't to be any emotional reunion and Louise set about sorting out Joyce's flat, as she'd promised. Maureen was helping her and together, they cleared out all the personal belongings, packing everything up for a local animal charity in line with

Joyce's wishes. As Maureen was putting the white eiderdown from Joyce's bed into a bag, they remembered the story of Joyce's kindness from long ago and thought it would make a lovely gift for Mary.

I had the chance to show Maureen a draft of this story when she came to visit recently. She had remained close to Mary right up until she'd died, just a few months ago and it seems we were mistaken about some of the details. There was no pram. Mary would never have been able to afford such a luxury. So she was carrying the baby past the flower shop with her mother, all those years ago.

The afternoon Maureen spent with Louise, clearing Joyce's flat had happened shortly before Mary was due to come home from hospital. Maureen had been getting her flat ready, doing some decorating and cleaning to make it cosy and welcoming and the idea of a new eiderdown fitted the project very well.

When she saw her bedroom again, Mary was delighted.

"Oh, Maureen! It's lovely. How much do I owe you for the new bedding?"

"Oh, no. It's alright. It's from Joyce's," said Maureen, explaining the connection.

"So where did Joyce live?" Mary asked her, the penny dropping slowly. "Not Joyce! Not Little Joyce from by the arches that had the florist's shop?"

"Yes, she had a flower shop,"

"Little Joyce? By the arches? In Ainbridge? That had the florist's shop?"

"Yes."

"She was the lady that … I couldn't afford a pram … She was the lady that watched me struggling with my little boy and on a cold day, she ran out with a blanket saying, 'your baby's going to get cold!' He was dressed but nothing to really keep him warm."

Evidently stirred by the memories, Mary smiled up at Maureen,

"And now Joyce is keeping me warm."

The intervening years had not been particularly kind to Mary. The relationship with her son had not flourished. After a long absence, twenty years or so, he reappeared and not, it seems, with the intention of seeking reconciliation at his mother's deathbed. But that's another whole story that we know nothing about. Our own story of Joyce and Mary is already sad enough yet somehow, it chimes with something in me, something about the importance of human connections and the value of small acts of kindness. In a long lifetime, how precious a tiny moment can be.

9 A WINTER'S TALE

Just at the beginning of the most severe winter on record, I arrived at the office one evening to find that Ann wasn't there yet. This was strange as she was always in first, sorting out the visits for the night. Then the phone rang. It was Bridget, from the other shift. She lives quite close to the office and she had seen a car on its side at the big roundabout near Asda. She thought it was Ann's car and was concerned that she might have been involved in an accident. Apparently, there was an ambulance already at the scene. So I thanked her and went straight to the roundabout. It's not far from the office and I was there in five minutes.

There was the car, definitely Ann's car, up on its side but there was no sign of Ann. The ambulance was still parked nearby so I knocked on the rear doors. A paramedic opened up and there was Ann inside, smiling out at me and fortunately unhurt. After checking her over, the paramedics offered to take her to hospital but she was able to reassure them that there was no need. She insisted she was OK and I took her back to the office.

To be honest, I was never particularly comfortable with

Ann's driving but I never said anything. You can't really, can you? There's a massive roundabout in Blem, a huge roundabout she used to go into at, probably fifty miles an hour and never took her foot off all the way round. Pinned against the passenger door and hanging on but trying not to make it too obvious, it felt like the Waltzers at the fairground. I've always thought, you just have to accept everybody's ways and differences. So I kept quiet and held on tight.

Anyway, back at the office, that was when the shock of it all came in. I could see she was still very shaken up and suggested it would be better if I took her home and she agreed. So we set about ringing round the nurses who lived closest to the office to see who could come in and take over our shift. No one hesitated. The first two nurses we called volunteered as soon as we explained the situation. These were the sort of people I had the honour and pleasure of working alongside for those twenty years.

§§§

Further on into the same winter, the conditions became even more severe with ice and snow and temperatures well below freezing. Being the evening shift, matters got worse as the night went on too. I think it was minus seventeen one evening, going home. It was that bad, the Health Authority stopped us using our own cars and provided drivers with four-wheel drive vehicles to pick each of us up from our homes, take us to the office to arrange all our visits and then drive us, staff nurse and auxiliary, in our usual pairs, to all our patients all over the county and finally deliver us home again. I felt like a rock star!

We still had a few anxious moments. I remember one incident with my heart in my mouth as we set off skidding down a country lane. Our driver seemed to be getting a bit ambitious, a touch over confident perhaps in his mighty four by four. He was obviously enjoying himself, well used to the vehicle and really owning it but … ooh! Still, he handled it, the car stayed on the road and we all lived to see another day.

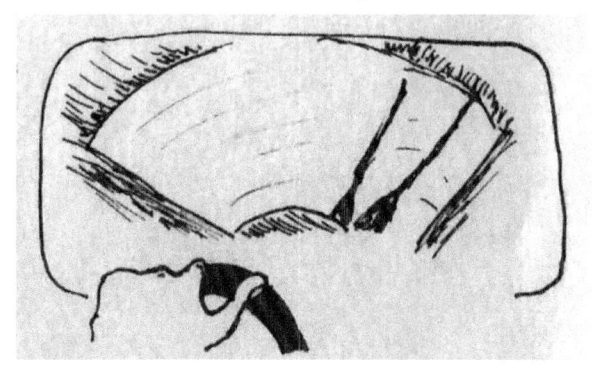

Even in the worst of weather, terminally ill patients still need their care and thanks to our skilful drivers we managed to reach all of them, every one, even in the most rural and isolated homes. I always knew our work was important but to have that extra support when we needed it was rewarding. It felt like recognition, like knowing the whole community was behind us, understanding how important it was too.

10 THE TIMES THEY ARE A-CHANGING

During my twenty years on the evening service I worked alongside so many amazing nurses, each one unique and special. In this story, I want to tell you about Pam, a staff nurse on our team, who came from southern Ireland.

Pam was going out alone one evening, on single patient visits. Her list included a lady who lived alone in a static caravan on a site in the wilds of Lancashire. (Oh God! Even now I can picture her walking in!) We'd finished our list and were already back in the office when she returned.

"What on earth, Pam?"

We couldn't believe the state of her, her uniform, her hair. It was back in the days when nurses had to wear dresses, before they were ever allowed to wear trousers and Pam looked as if she had been dragged through a hedge and back again.

"Whatever happened?"

In her lilting voice, she started to explain.

"Fookin' hell!" she began in her musical, Irish accent.

"You wouldn't believe what I had to do!"

Arriving at the site, there had been no reply when she knocked at the door of the caravan. So she had walked around to look through the windows and see what she could see and there was the lady lying on the floor inside the caravan. Luckily, Pam spotted a small top window open and, being quite slight and agile, thought she might manage to climb up and wriggle through. After a lot of twisting, pushing and pulling, she dropped onto the floor and was able to start attending to her patient.

The lady had fallen and was unable to get up but she didn't seem to have been injured. She assured Pam that, with a little help, if she could just get back into her chair, everything would be OK. And that's what happened. Pam managed to help the lady up from the floor and into her chair and left her with a cup of tea which seemed to make everything fine. Appreciating the warm thanks and reassurances of her patient, Pam, straightened her tattered uniform as best she could and went on her way.

§§§

I'm not sure that this sort of ... what is it? Dedication?

Commitment? Resourcefulness? Whatever it is, I don't think it's so easy to find these days. I mean no disrespect to the nurses still working today. So much seems to have changed in so little time. I don't think the modern NHS allows them the sort of independence we used to have.

There's sure to be a 'correct procedure' for 'unable to access the patient's accommodation' and it won't include scrambling in through the window. It wouldn't surprise me if Pam would have been disciplined if she'd gone in through the window today. She'd probably have to call the Police. And what about leaving such a vulnerable patient alone? And in a caravan? Would today's nurses be left to use their own judgement for such a decision? Or might they be fearful of an inquiry if the lady is later found to have died there, alone?

So much changed in my time on the District. Val retired five years before me. She was of the age when women could still retire at sixty while I went on to sixty-five. It was getting to the point where she was starting to be stretched to the limit of how she could move with the modern ways and the computers and I was the same.

The manager always used to say to me,

> "Ben! Your inbox! There's five hundred emails. Can you clear them!"

What was I doing with five hundred emails? What was I even doing with an inbox? Everything, any little course, any information from the main hospitals used to come into our emails as well; absolutely irrelevant to the job.

> "Ben! Can you please clear your emails!"

I felt cornered. Did I mention I was a joiner? To be honest, I wasn't particularly confident about how to switch the computer on.

"Look!" I said.

(What was the manager's name? I can't remember. She was lovely ... Linda! It was Linda ... but she didn't understand my situation and I thought I was going to be 'found out'!)

"Look, Linda! I'm sorry but there's only one computer in this office and the staff nurses have priority over it. What chance have I got? When am I supposed to work on my emails?"

It was true and she knew it. I can still remember the tension I felt and the relief as I started to think I might have got away with it ... but it was an uncomfortable moment. Of course, the team came to the rescue, as usual.

"Don't worry, Ben," said Ann. "I'll clear them for you, one night when we're back early."

And she did but me and Val, we were on the same wavelength. Change was overtaking us and we were in a young person's world now. The experience of life and of the job didn't count any more. I don't think they'll still be taking on any forty five year old joiners these days. The new technology and the new management somehow took away the personal side.

We were put on a lifting and handling course every single year where we wondered why we were doing it. Because we were doing it year after year after year and thinking, well, we've done it. It's all the same. Everything was the same. I think it changed once, from an Australian lift. They stopped it. I found it was a real good lift with two of you but for some reason, we had to stop using it.

I had an altercation with the instructor one year. I had to highlight the difference between the classroom and the situations in most peoples' homes. In class we had an adjustable bed and plenty of room to move around. The average double bed is low down, so you have to get your knee in and there's no pumping up of the bed. It could even be somebody sleeping on a sofa with a big hard back where it's impossible to have another person on the other side.

But it was to cover claims really. They'd say, if you injured your back,

"Were you not doing the lift like we showed you?"

Naturally, we'd always say,

"Of course we were!"

But nurses were still lifting and still hurting their backs.

In the end, they stopped physical lifting altogether. It was slide sheets we had, for sliding the patient. We had our reservations but we had to go with it. It was a great idea but if you've got a patient with a pressure sore and you're sliding them on that pressure sore, you're making it worse. So it was 'swings and roundabouts' but you had to go with it.

I suppose, ninety per cent of the time, they were good. Such a simple idea too, plastic slide sheets. There was one blue and one red. I can't remember now what the difference was but the main one we used was blue. They were supposed to be put into every house, with all the equipment for nursing a person at home but we always carried one in the car, just in case.

The whole job did change dramatically in quite a short time and I can see it needed to. We used to hold the patient up, the full weight of a sixteen or eighteen stone person, in a line, three of us, while another one washed underneath and dried and changed the sheet, quick as they could.

Yes, it changed dramatically and for the better but as far as the technology was concerned, it overtook me and Val and we got out just in time. After I'd finished, I remember seeing Ann some time later.

> "Crikey! You wouldn't believe it," she said. "There's no writing now. There's no 'Cardex'. There's no reports. They don't have a 'Nurses' Notes' in the house any more. It's all done on tablets."

It seemed to me, even while I was still there, as the service became more 'professional', it also became less personal, less human.

§§§

But I'm starting to wander. Back to Pam! She was involved in another dramatic story some months later. It wasn't about the nursing or the patient this time. It was just another of those surprising things that can turn up and make life so amazing.

"If I don't tell you, you won't know!"

Pam was visiting a lady in warden-controlled accommodation. On the way to the patient's flat, she walked past a communal lounge and heard music pouring out. A gentleman was entertaining the residents, playing a keyboard and having a good old sing-along.

The visit was uneventful and brief so she soon said goodbye to the patient and headed back towards her car, passing the communal lounge again. This time she was surprised by silence. The music and singing had stopped and there was the musician, slumped over his keyboard with the horrified residents looking on in shock.

Having to take charge of the situation once again, she ran across, lifted the man onto the floor and checked his pulse. She immediately started giving him chest compressions and mouth-to-mouth resuscitation. One of the residents pressed the alarm for the warden on duty who called for an ambulance. Pam carried on giving CPR until the ambulance arrived and the paramedics took over.

"Well done, Nurse! We have a pulse. It looks as if he will live."

Sure enough, about a month later the warden telephoned to tell us the musician was back with his keyboard, playing and singing along with the residents. The communal lounge was ringing with music again.

So that's another story with a happy ending, thanks to Pam. Eventually, she and her family moved back to southern Ireland to live. That was our loss and their gain - an amazing nurse.

11 "IF I DON'T TELL YOU, YOU WON'T KNOW"

Ah, what a lot of happy memories. I'm suddenly remembering the elderly patient with diabetes and his wife. Half past eleven or quarter to twelve at night and only two more patients to see to before home and bed.

We'd taken a call from a GP as we were getting our list of visits together. An elderly man in his mid-nineties had been into the surgery for his regular blood sugar check. The doctor had been a little concerned over his reading and could we recheck it as late as possible that evening? So we added him on, near the end of the list and by eleven thirty, we'd seen them all apart from him and another elderly patient in a residential care home. Checking blood sugar level doesn't take long. It was looking good for finishing on time (or so we thought!)

The elderly gentleman opened the door himself and showed us through to the kitchen where his wife, Agnes, was sitting at the table. They were aware that we'd had to leave him as late as possible and they were expecting us and had been waiting patiently. Agnes smiled pleasantly and said hello. As it turned out, that was the only word we would hear from her.

The test quickly showed that the gentleman's blood sugar was back to a satisfactory level and no further treatment was needed. We were done and off to the care home for our last patient. Then, just as we were packing up, he said,

> "Now, I know you're in a rush but if I don't tell you, you won't know."

We looked up.

> "When me and Agnes came out of the doctor's surgery this afternoon … We know of the best café just across the road that makes the best bacon butty in Ormsley, doesn't it, Agnes?"

Agnes gave a little nod of her head.

> "Now I know you're busy but if I don't tell you, you won't know. So we sat down with our cup of tea and butties, best butties money can buy, aren't they, Agnes?"

Another nod from Agnes.

> "So there we were, enjoying our bacon butties when all of a sudden, I brought the whole lot back up, all over the table, didn't I Agnes?"

And another nod.

We always tried to give everyone as much time as we thought they needed but professionally, so we could get to the next patient promptly, more or less when we were expected. It was never easy, balancing the needs of the patients and their carers for some compassion and support against the demands of the clock.

> "Well, we knew it wasn't the bacon butty. We've had

many a bacon butty at this café and I was never sick before, was I, Agnes?"

Never a word from Agnes. He only needed the nod. He was on a roll. We had a little window into their whole way of life; the storyteller and the silent one.

"That right, Agnes?"

Just a look and a nod.

"Now, I know you're busy but if I don't tell you, you won't know. So we just managed to get the bus home, just got through the door when I was sick again, wasn't I Agnes?"

We turned to Agnes for the confirmation, then back to the patient for the next piece, bit like Wimbledon.

"But I'm alright now, aren't I, Agnes?"

Yes. Agnes agrees. He's alright now. He was someone you couldn't walk away from and say,

"Look, look! I'm sorry but we really do have to go."

No. We were going to be held until he was done. I was so glad it was Ann I was working with that night. Now, if it had been Kath, with the short fuse, it would have been a different story. He wouldn't have got through it. She'd have cut him off somehow.

As it was, Ann and I were looking at each other wondering, when is this going to end? Finally, he turned to us and said,

"If I didn't tell you, you wouldn't have known."

We were released.

When you can just give people that little bit more time, the things you can learn, the understanding … and the humour. He was so entertaining. I laughed from their front door, all the way to the nursing home where we were going next. Luckily, it was Ann's night to drive so I didn't have to. I couldn't stop laughing.

"D'you know, Ann? That's finished the night brilliantly. What a gem!"

Aren't I lucky to have been through all that?

12 JUST WHEN YOU THOUGHT THE NIGHT WAS OVER!

The drama of the evening didn't always end with the shift. Driving about in the small hours of the morning, across the rural wilds of West Prestonshire was itself an adventure. I never quite knew what might be turning up around the next corner.

At about one o'clock in the morning, on the way home after a particularly busy night, I was rounding a sharp bend when I saw two young men standing in the road, waving me down. I stopped to see what they wanted and before I was even out of my car, I noticed another car on its side in the ditch at the edge of the road.

"Is anybody injured," I asked the lads as I got out?

"No, we're OK."

It turned out there were four of them, young farmers on a night out, going too fast and misjudging the bend on the way home and lucky to come out of it unhurt.

"Could you drop us off at the farm? It's only about five miles away. We want to get the tractor so we can pull the car out."

They were in a bit of a panic to get it all sorted out without the police turning up and needing an explanation. But they came across as pretty responsible lads, well-behaved and in control. As it happened, the farm was on my route home anyway, so the four young men climbed into the car. They couldn't thank me enough, chatting away all along the journey until I dropped them off at the farm to get the tractor.

As I went round the same sharp bend the following night, the car was gone, so for the young farmers, it must have been mission accomplished.

§§§

In the early hours after the shift, winding home along the quiet rural lanes, it was a good time for spotting wildlife. I had many charming surprises. Once my headlights caught four dog-like creatures, jumping up and down on the road as if they were dancing on hot coals.

Coming closer, I saw they were fox cubs, obviously discovering a hard, asphalt road surface for the first time and confused by what their little paws were feeling. It was a wonderful sight to see, these four little fox cubs, wondering what they had stepped onto for the first time.

There was another memorable time I was surprised by a family of foxes in the middle of the night. About half way home, sweeping round a bend, my headlights caught two adult foxes with their cubs, walking along in the middle of the road. They were completely blocking my way, taking their time, as though they were on their regular, nightly errands. They weren't a bit bothered about the car moving slowly behind them.

> "Hey! Hang on! Just a minute," I seemed to hear. "I've got my family here. This is our time. You shouldn't be around at this time in the morning. What do you think you're doing?"

It was amazing. I just crawled behind them. I couldn't get past because they were splayed all across the road. Two adult foxes, mother and father, I suppose and I think there were four or six cubs. It was just like they were out for the night's stroll. There was no panic, nothing. It was a just a stroll. And that was the funniest part, the way ... it must have been the mother or the father, at the front, turned round and looked at me, then just led them off, into the field, all in their own time.

Magic little moments that I never expect to see again, probably.

§§§

But it wasn't always foxes. I never knew what the next surprise was going to be. Once it was a lady stepping out and waving her arms as I was driving over the old, stone, canal bridge. I pulled over.

> "Our car won't start. Could you possibly give us a push?"

By the canal at the side of the bridge is a parking area for fishermen or walkers using the canal path but at one o'clock in the morning, I don't think they were fishing or walking. (He-he!)

Anyway, I always carry a set of jump leads with me in case of a breakdown so I was glad enough to pull alongside their car to help. A very embarrassed gentleman climbed out and thanked me for stopping. We quickly hooked up the batteries and got them started and I watched a pink-faced couple drive off into the night, presumably to their separate homes. That's just how it came across. They both shouldn't have been there and they weren't young either, well into their forties. It was obviously naughty times. (There's hope for us all, eh?)

Another late night sighting had me quite confused and concerned for a while. Luckily, I had been working with Ann and she was following just behind me in her car. In my usual, middle-of-the-night, daydream, half way round a big roundabout on the dual carriageway, I was startled by an apparition.

Glaring in the headlights suddenly was the biggest, whitest bottom I'd ever seen. An overweight man was mooning at me on the roundabout at one o'clock in the morning. When you're very tired after a long busy shift, your mind can play tricks and by the time I got home, I thought I must have imagined it.

I told Ann when I saw her the following night, I thought I must have been seeing things as I'd imagined an overweight man with his huge white bottom, mooning on the roundabout at one o'clock in the morning.

> "No, no," she said. "You weren't seeing things. I was right behind you. I saw him there too, in the headlights, huge white bottom and all, on the roundabout at one o'clock in the morning."

So we weren't going crazy, imagining things which weren't there. We really saw a big white bottom on the roundabout at one o'clock in the morning.

Who on earth would do that, on his own, at that time in the morning? What was he thinking? What did he say to himself, when he got home?

"Yesss! I've done it! I finally got two! One car after the other!"

13 PARTING THOUGHTS

As I've said already, with the majority of our patients being terminally ill, I became rather familiar with death during my twenty years on the evening service. I am so grateful for that experience. It has left me completely unafraid. I think it's sad that we seem to find it so difficult to face death. It's such a huge part of life and yet, until it confronts us directly, we mostly look the other way.

Approaching the end, most patients would be on a syringe driver pump to administer their drugs and a catheter to keep them dry and these have to be removed after they've passed away. For any patient in our area of all West Prestonshire, if they died on our shift, we were on call to go and take down the equipment, destroy the drugs, tidy the patient up and make them presentable, as much as we could.

It was a normal and unpredictable part of our job, another reason why we never knew what was going to come at us on any given night. It wasn't just nursing our patients while they were alive but also taking care of them after they died and if they died while we were out and about we'd get the call. The family always had our number to ring.

"Mr Johnson or Mrs Tibbert has died. Can you come?"

It was a special part of the job too. There was something about those calls when we knew the struggle was over and the pain finally stopped. It also meant we had the chance to say goodbye to the family as well as the patient. You can get really close when you've been visiting a long time.

So we'd get the call and we'd have to go. I always liked to get there as quickly as possible. It was one of my pet things. I hated leaving them with their mouths wide open. Straight away, when they die, you can close their mouth easily and it'll stay there but sometimes, as much as we'd try to be quick, it might've been an hour or more and that was too long. You couldn't get the mouth to close properly.

I hated leaving them like that. I used to wedge a pillow right under their chin, as tight as I could. I even used to push it there as strong as I could and hold their mouth shut for as long as I could, while Ann or Val was carrying on with the cleaning and taking the catheter out. If the patient has died with their mouth open, there was nothing worse ... to try and give them some dignity and get them looking as presentable as possible for the family.

It could be a bit awkward because families did have their favourites. There was a time when it was me and Ann, towards the last few years, when Val had retired. Who were the other two? There was Kath, the scouser who was a bit short of patience and a young auxiliary from Lembridge ... a lovely girl.

You see, close to the end, it was like a call-out. They'd call and say,

> "My husband's really poorly. Do you think you could come?"

So we'd go and they'd say,

> "Oh! I'm so glad it's you."

It's a bit naughty but it was a great satisfaction to know our support was appreciated. It seemed little enough to us in the face of their difficulties and their sadness. We almost always found ourselves saying, we wished we could have done more. So it was lovely when this certain patient's wife invited us, as a thank-you, for a meal at the Saracen's Head in Tilsley but they only asked me and Ann.

> "Oh no. What are we going to do? How are we going to deal with this?"

Ann thought we'd have to go, out of respect. She was a lovely person, the wife that was left.

> "So we'll go and just not say we've been. They don't have to know … and we'll just hope it doesn't come out."

So we did. We took potluck and I don't think they ever did find out.

For all the sadness, it was always a special time when a person had just passed away. I was aware of a change in the atmosphere of their room. I can only describe it as a beautiful, serene, calm energy. It was the same for every patient we attended on their passing, through all my years with the Service, that serene, calm atmosphere. I've never experienced a feeling like it, anywhere else or at any other time, either before I started nursing or since I have retired.

All the nurses spoke about it and every one said the same, a beautiful, peaceful atmosphere, hard to describe or explain. Only, we all agreed, for it to have been such a gift to have seen that moment of life ending, to have heard death come and go. So many times I saw it, over those twenty years. I'm so glad that we were able to bring some comfort to the families as they suffered their loss. I remember every one.

I feel great warmth and peace from having such a personal experience of death and I have no fear. I can see how precious every month is, every week, every day. Each morning you wake up and you're not hit with disease or debilitating health conditions, you or your family, you've got the best day of your life. That's what's made me so grateful for every minute.

14 RETIREMENT

After twenty years on the District Nurses Evening Service, at the age of sixty five, I retired and it was shortly after that, Louise and I paid a visit to her sister Diane in Scotland. One evening, while we were chatting with Diane and her husband, Frank, Louise said to me, tell them the story about that unbelievable night, that visit to the cottage by the canal, the one that ended up taking all night. So I started trying to remember all the scenarios that unfolded that night, one after the other, funny episodes and alarming incidents, heart breaking and heart warming.

"You've got a tricky situation here!"

"You don't say!"

Back home, a couple of weeks later, my story came back to me, all typed up in an email to Louise and with some helpful comments and questions. Unknown to me, Frank had recorded the story and transcribed it for me, with names changed for anonymity. He said I should collect my stories together.

"They're precious; stories about ordinary people at their most vulnerable, told with such love and respect that we are reminded, in case we might have forgotten, that we are all special. Nobody is 'ordinary'."

So with Frank's enthusiasm and encouragement behind me, I started to remember and write down all these true stories from everyday life on the West Prestonshire District Nurses Evening Service. I hope you enjoy reading them as much as I've enjoyed telling them.

POST SCRIPT

A few months on from finishing my book, Louise and I moved house. Going through all the boxes, Louise came across an old get-well card to me. It was from two patients I'd had the pleasure of nursing nearly twenty years before: Philip, who was suffering from motor neurone disease (MND) and his wife, Jenny who cared for him.

Confined to a wheelchair, he was totally reliant on her but they were determined to make the best of the life they had. So they invested in a specially adapted vehicle, big enough to take Philip in his wheelchair and equipped with a ramp and hoist to haul him in.

Before he became ill, Philip was a keen golfer and had been captain of the local club in his day. So Jenny, always caring and determined, would make sure he got to any dinners or functions at the club, driving him there, staying for the duration and driving him home to their lovely stone cottage in the countryside.

Life seemed pretty good until a second, cruel blow struck. Jenny was diagnosed with an aggressive form of cancer and we ended up nursing both of them together. I was proud to be a part of that team. Along with the daytime district nurses and the overnight Marie Curie nurses, we supported Philip and Jenny so they were able to stay in their beautiful home until Philip died a few months later and Jenny moved into a hospice for the last few weeks of her life. They were such a devoted couple.

During that time, while we were nursing them both, I had a spell in hospital myself, for a hip replacement. My operation was on the fifth of November, Bonfire Night and as I lay in bed in the recovery ward, listening to the fireworks going off outside, I remember thinking, "I can not believe that the name of my surgeon is Mr Fawkes."

The other reason for the smile on my face was a 'get-well' card from Philip and Jenny. Val brought it to the hospital when she came to visit. Even with all the stress and heartache of their own, terrible situation, they thought of me and took the time to buy a card to cheer me up. This is what they wrote:

> Dear Ben.
>
> We are so pleased to hear you are progressing well and that Mr Fawkes did not blow you up on November 5th. Philip and I are both missing your evening calls and look forward to seeing you fit and well. Our very good wishes to you for a speedy recovery.
>
> Love Philip & Jenny.

Do you see what I'm getting at? The selflessness and kindness of people, with their own suffering and all that they have to deal with: it just sums up the privilege I feel, to have met such beautiful people on my journey. Thank you Philip and Jenny. I hope this story pays tribute to two more, very kind and courageous human beings.

ABOUT THE AUTHOR

Ben Parbold has worked all his life as a joiner, improving the properties of Westport, Prestonshire since the 1960s. Happier with trowel, hammer or saw in hand than pen, he is nonetheless setting out on his third career as a writer with these touching tales from his remarkable second career as a nurse.

Ben is a Ju-Jitsu master and keen gardener and lives in Westport with his wife, Louise and Cavapoo, Bonny.

Printed in Great Britain
by Amazon